NICHOLAS SU

C000243784

MEDICINE AND HEALTH CARE IN ROMAN BRITAIN

SHIRE ARCHAEOLOGY

Front cover:
The Roman military hospital at Housesteads on Hadrian's Wall. (©English Heritage)

British Library Cataloguing in Publication Data: Summerton, Nicholas. Medicine and health care in Roman Britain. – (Shire archaeology; 87) 1. Medicine, Greek and Roman 2. Romans – Great Britain – Health and hygiene 3. Medicine – Great Britain – History – To 1500 4. Public health – Great Britain – History – To 1500 5. Great Britain – History – Roman period, 55 B.C.– 449 A.D. I. Title 610.9'361 ISBN-13: 978 0 7478 0664 6.

Published in 2007 by
SHIRE PUBLICATIONS LTD
Cromwell House, Church Street, Princes Risborough,
Buckinghamshire HP27 9AA, UK.
(Website: www.shirebooks.co.uk)

Series Editor: James Dyer.

ISBN 978 0 7478 0664 6.

Number 87 in the Shire Archaeology series.

First published 2007.

Printed in Malta by Gutenberg Press Ltd, Gudja Road, Tarxien PLA 19, Malta.

Contents

List of illustrations

Acknowledgements

In developing this book I am indebted to a large number of individuals stretching back over twenty years. However, I should like to express my particular thanks to Ralph Jackson, Barry Cunliffe, Audrey Cruse, Bill Putnam, Keith Manchester, Michael Jones and David Tomalin. I am also very grateful to the staff of Shire Publications for their helpful suggestions and guidance.

Others have generously provided me with illustrations and I should also like to thank Lord Bledisloe for permitting me access to the site at Lydney.

Above all, I must express my gratitude to my parents, Barry and June, my wife, Ailie, and my three daughters, Katrina, Siân and Emily, for patiently accompanying me on my numerous forays in search of Roman Britain.

Figures 6, 17, 22 and 23 are © The British Museum and are reproduced with permission; figures 3, 9 and 13 are © Guy de la Bédoyère and are reproduced with permission; figures 18, 35, 37 and the front cover illustration are © English Heritage and are reproduced with permission; figure 20 is © The Vindolanda Trust and is reproduced with permission. I am also grateful to the following for allowing me to reproduce their images: Chester Museum (figures 1 and 2), Mark Hassall and the Roman Society (figure 8), Dr G. Hart and Lord Bledisloe (figure 14), Newport Museum (Bruce Campbell) (figure 21), Norwich Museum (Tim Pestell) (figure 26), Brading Roman Villa (figure 27), Bill Putnam (figure 33), Michael Jones (figure 30), John Wacher (figure 31) and The Lord Barnard (figure 17). I am also very grateful to Miss Siân Summerton for her drawings of the Littleborough forceps (figure 24).

1
Introduction

There can be little doubt that the Romano-Britons experienced many of the illnesses that are encountered today by general practitioners. Each individual would also have had to decide how best to deal with their health-related concern. Today some patients might consult their doctor as soon as they experience back pain, but most are more likely to use a home remedy, discuss it with a close friend or relative, visit the pharmacist or even consider a complementary therapist. Similarly, although the range of treatment opportunities would have been different for the Romano-British patient, individual choice would still have played an important part in determining the type of care selected.

However, in considering medicine in Roman Britain it is crucial not to become blinkered by a modern perspective: health and health care must always be seen in context. For example, a condition considered 'normal' in one society (or at one time) might represent a medical problem in other circumstances. Currently in the United Kingdom low blood pressure is generally not treated but elsewhere in Europe the situation is different. Furthermore, illnesses that are considered to warrant the input of a doctor nowadays might, at other times, have been very effectively dealt with by other healers. By adopting a twenty-first-century view it is also all too easy to dismiss or denigrate some aspects of ancient medicine and yet to overplay others significantly. How can we be confident that a bronze instrument was actually a surgical tool? Do aqueducts, drains and bath-houses really reflect a concern for the public health? Should we so easily dismiss dream therapy and other apparently bizarre treatments as being ineffective in the context of Roman Britain?

In considering medicine and health care in Roman Britain it would also be wrong to ignore the influences consequent on being part of the wider Roman Empire. Roman medicine was essentially an amalgam of theories and practices derived from the indigenous inhabitants of Rome, the Etruscans, the Egyptians and the Greeks, among others. The Greek impact on Roman medicine was particularly dominant and Greek medical theories, translated into Latin, continued to be studied and applied in Europe for over thirteen hundred years after the demise of the Western Roman Empire.

At the time of the Roman invasion of Britain four major medical sects or schools (all with Greek origins) were prevalent within Rome: Dogmatics, Empiricists, Pneumatists and Methodists. The Dogmatics believed in the importance of logical thinking in identifying underlying causes of diseases. Many emphasised that it was critical to seek to maintain an appropriate balance between the four 'cardinal humours' identified by Hippocrates, i.e. blood, yellow bile, black bile, and phlegm, in securing good health. Restoring the equilibrium involved such therapies as blood letting, the use of emetics such as hellebore, and specific diets. The Pneumatists were a splinter group of the Dogmatics and placed great emphasis on the *pneuma* or spirit as the controlling factor in health and disease. The followers of this school considered that good *pneuma* could be maintained by careful attention to the environment, such as house design, water supply and bathing. In contrast to the Dogmatics and the Pneumatists, the Empiricists argued that careful observation of the patient and his or her symptoms was imperative. Moreover, treatments should be determined by what had been effective before in similar circumstances and Empiricist physicians were less concerned about underlying causes of ill health.

Of the four schools Methodism was possibly the most dominant throughout the Roman world. What made it particularly attractive to the average Roman was its focus on practical therapies rather than complicated theories. The founder of the sect, Asclepiades, came to Rome from Bithynia (modern north-west Turkey) in 91 BC and championed five types of basic therapy: regulating the intake of food and wine, massage, exercise, rocking appliances (to provide passive exercise for those unable to indulge in more strenuous activity), and bathing. The Methodists also dismissed the theory of humours, and venesection, in particular, was rejected as a treatment.

Ninety-five per cent of doctors recorded on inscriptions from Italy and the Western Latin provinces of the Empire before AD 100 bore Greek names. As will be discussed in this book, there is evidence for Greek influences within Roman Britain, although, in relation to the medical theories being followed, it is important to note that no cupping vessel (used for bleeding in keeping with the humoral ideologies) has ever been identified from Britain. Non-Greek medical finds from Romano-British contexts include an Egyptian haematite amulet from near Welwyn in Hertfordshire, inscribed with a representation of the uterus, a scarab beetle and the name 'Ororiouth', a protector spirit against women's diseases. At Bath the presence of the haruspex Lucius Marcius Memor suggests Etruscan influences on medical care. Haruspication involved slaughtering an animal, usually a sheep, and carefully examining and 'reading' the liver and intestines. It was suggested that specific aspects of the health of the person bringing the sacrifice could be determined from the anatomy of the animal's internal organs.

Owing to the work of authors such as Celsus, Pliny, Dioscorides, Scribonius Largus and Galen, knowledge about treatments would have been spread widely across the empire. Scribonius Largus listed

271 recipes and mentions 249 vegetable, forty-five mineral and thirty-six animal substances. Galen assembled six hundred remedies, Pliny nine hundred and Dioscorides just over one thousand substances, of which about seven hundred are plants. However, what is particularly interesting is that these writers cite treatments from Britain, suggesting a good pharmacological communication network across the empire. For example, the writer Dioscorides was familiar with the medical uses of British mead in addition to plants from his native areas around Tarsus. Among his eye remedies Galen includes a mercuric collyrium developed by Axius, '*opthalmikos* of the British Fleet'. Pliny even mentions a plant called *Britannica*, which was most likely dock and used for treating scurvy. Moreover, the lid of a lead pot found at the Roman fort of Haltern in Germany was inscribed with the words *EX RADICE BRITANICA*, translated as 'extract of the root of *Britannica*'.

The identification of surgical instruments from Roman Britain relies heavily on analogous finds from elsewhere in the Roman Empire, complemented by descriptions from the classical medical authors. Particularly significant are finds from graves or the so-called 'disaster' sites at Rimini, Pompeii and Herculanium, where a catastrophic event has led to *in situ* preservation of medical tools. In AD 257–8 the Almanni attacked and looted the northern part of Italy, including the small Roman town at Rimini. One of the houses they burnt had belonged to a doctor and, because the building was subsequently simply covered over, the contents were preserved. Excavations in 1989 brought to light over 150 instruments, including thirty-two relating to bone surgery, seven dental forceps and an array of scalpels, surgical knives, forceps, needles, hooks and probes. The small set of instruments carried by one of the victims of the eruption of Vesuvius at Pompeii (presumably also a doctor) comprised four scalpels, two forceps, two hooks, six probes and two needles. The extensive range of probes found in most circumstances perhaps reflects inadequacies in anatomical knowledge among Roman doctors due to constraints on human dissection within the Roman world.

However, in considering medicine and health care in Roman Britain such empire-wide influences must be balanced against local circumstances and modifications. Furthermore, although we know something of the Greek medical theories circulating in Rome, no information is available about the pre-Roman local health beliefs prevalent in Iron Age Britain before the arrival of the Romans.

In relation to treatments, Celsus stated (*Prooemium* 30) that 'methods of practice differ according to the nature of localities, and that one method is required in Rome, another in Egypt, another in Gaul'. For example, collyrium stamps, used for impressing the name of the maker and the purposes of a treatment on to a hardened block of eye ointment (collyrium), are found only in Gaul, Germania and Britannia. Whether this reflects differences in diseases, medical systems, fiscal arrangements or simply the practicalities of managing medicines is a matter of continuing debate.

In relation to the religious aspects of medicine and health (see chapter 3), Julius Caesar regarded Apollo (as opposed to Aesculapius) as the main healing deity of the Celtic tribes in Gaul. In Britain archaeological evidence from a number of sites such as Nettleton (Wiltshire) and Wroxeter (Shropshire) suggests that Apollo was also widely worshipped in Roman Britain in addition to Aesculapius. There was also some cross-fertilisation between Roman and British deities: at Bath the Roman Minerva (Medica) was amalgamated with the Celtic healing goddess Sulis, and at Corbridge in Northumberland Salus (the Roman goddess of health) was associated with the Celtic goddess Brigantia.

The distance from Rome and the time taken for new ideas to spread might also have had an influence on the 'medical fashions' in the provinces. Votives were a special form of remuneration given to the gods for their services to mankind. When a supplicant had vowed to give a particular payment in return for having a request fulfilled the gift became an ex-voto. Votives were made from a variety of materials and took various forms, including anatomical models of body parts, tools, weapons and figurines, as well as dedications and written testimonies. Anatomical votives were often given to the various healing deities of the ancient world but, by the first century BC, the custom had almost died out in Italy, whereas in Gaul and Britain there is evidence that the practice continued. For example, five thousand first-century AD wooden votives representing arms, heads, torsos and sexual organs have been found at the natural spring of the Source des Roches in a suburb of Clermont-Ferrand in France. In Britain, the finds from Lydney (Gloucestershire) and Wroxeter date to even later.

Much of the evidence relating to medicine and health care in Roman Britain has been assembled and is critically examined in this book.

2
The medical personnel

Doctors

When the emperor Claudius crossed the English Channel in the early days of the Roman invasion of Britain he was accompanied by two doctors, Caius Xenophon and Scribonius Largus. Xenophon, Claudius' personal physician, was subsequently given the title *praefectus fabrum* but proved rather ungrateful for the honour lavished on him, as, according to Tacitus, he eventually helped Claudius to his end: 'while pretending to help Claudius to vomit, he put a feather dipped in a quick poison down his throat. Xenophon knew that major crimes, though hazardous to undertake, are profitable to achieve' (*Annals* XII, 66).

Scribonius Largus had a particular interest in pharmacology, publishing his *Drug Recipes* in AD 47. He was always looking out for new treatments and in one of his 271 recipes he describes a herb found near Luni in Etruria while waiting to embark with the emperor's household troops en route for Britain.

Other emperors, governors and men of substance who visited and lived in Roman Britain would, presumably, also have been accompanied by their personal physicians. The emperor Septimus Severus, who is said to have suffered badly from gout, certainly had two doctors in attendance upon him during his Scottish campaign. On the return of the emperor to York, the physicians received instructions from the emperor's son, Caracalla, that they should seek to hasten the death of Septimus Severus. Their refusal was disastrous for them and it is possible that their remains are among the beheaded skeletons unearthed at York in 2005.

However, it is important to appreciate that these elite doctors, although well remembered in the historical record, represented a very small and select group. Even Galen, the personal physician to the emperor Marcus Aurelius, and from whom much of our understanding of Roman medicine is derived, would probably have had very little in common with the 'doctors' encountered by the average Romano-Briton.

For many Romans the concept of a personal professional physician was an anathema. It was at odds with the traditional Roman values of self-sufficiency and looking after your own. As mentioned in the introduction, the vast majority of the doctors in the Western Roman Empire were Greek or of Greek descent, and Romans were often highly suspicious of such individuals. On some Roman farms it seems that the head of the household (*pater familias*) also performed the role of chief healer, with responsibility for the health of his family and any estate workers. One of the writing tablets found at Vindolanda on Hadrian's

Wall indicates that the women of military families were expected to deal with the day-to-day health problems that arose in their households and that they kept a selection of medicines to hand for this purpose. In letter 294 Paterna appears to promise to supply Lepidina with two remedies, one of which was for fever.

From a modern perspective, an additional problem is to clarify what led to an individual acquiring the title 'doctor'. There were no medical schools, no examinations and no professional licensing procedures in the Roman world. A doctor was simply an individual who claimed the title and carried out treatment for some type of remuneration. Galen completed twelve years of study in order to build the foundations of his career. Some doctors worked as apprentices for a period of time but there was no barrier to others simply setting themselves up in practice with a very minimal level of training. Even if we assume that the medical works of Celsus and Galen circulated in Britain, there is no guarantee that they were read (or even could be read) by the local doctors.

There were occasional attempts at regulation of the medical profession within the Roman Empire by offering tax advantages or civic salaries. For example, in Roman Egypt there is evidence that tax privileges could be obtained by making a declaration before a magistrate (probably accompanied by some form of testimonial) that the individual was a *bone fide* doctor. However, for many, treating a famous patient was probably the most effective mechanism for gaining a reputation and the status of a doctor.

There is epigraphic evidence for the presence of physicians in Roman Britain. Two altars inscribed in Greek and dedicated by doctors have been found in Chester. The inscriptions are translated as: 'To the mighty Saviour Gods, I, Hermogenes, a doctor, set up this altar' (figure 1); 'The doctor Antiochus honours the all-surpassing saviours of men among the immortals. Aesculapius of the gentle hands,

1. An altar found at Chester, inscribed in Greek and dedicated by the doctor Hermogenes. (Photograph: Chester Museum)

2. An altar found at Chester and inscribed poetically in Greek to Aesculapius, Hygeia and Panakeia by the doctor Antiochus. (Photograph: Chester Museum)

Hygeia and Panakeia' (figure 2).

Both altars were found within the area of the military fortress and close to a building whose design resembles that of a Roman legionary hospital (see chapter 5). The text on the altar by Antiochus was particularly poetic, perhaps an attempt to emphasise his educated status. However, whether Hermogenes and Antiochus were legionary doctors, civilian doctors or, perhaps, personal physicians to senior officials remains uncertain. Intriguingly, Hadrian's personal physician was also called Hermogenes.

A third-century altar commemorating a doctor and inscribed in Latin has also been found at Binchester (County Durham) (figure 3): 'To Aesculapius and Salus for the welfare of the Cavalry Regiment of Vettonians, Roman citizens, Marcus Aurelius [...]ocomas, doctor, willingly and deservedly fulfilled his vow.' His names are incomplete but the first two, Marcus Aurelius, indicate that he was a Roman citizen, though not of very long standing, while the third, imperfectly preserved, is of Greek origin.

It has been suggested that the more skilled and educated Greek doctors such as Hermogenes, Antiochus and Marcus Aurelius may have moved back and forth between civilian and military practice. If this were the case

3. A third-century altar from Binchester (County Durham) dedicated to Aesculapius and Salus by the doctor Marcus Aurelius. (© Guy de la Bédoyère)

then they would not have been bound by the usual terms of enlistment for twenty or twenty-five years.

Military medics

Roman Britain always had a strong military presence and, in addition to the occasional Greek doctor, a range of medical assistance would have been available to the front-line soldiers. At the sharp end were the *capsarii*, the medical orderlies or dressers, the name being derived from the round bandage box (*capsa*) that they carried. They were probably ordinary soldiers concerned mainly with the first aid necessary during battle. Some may have been *immunes*, with their medical work being deemed important enough to allow them to be excluded from regular duties. Furthermore, it seems that the *capsarii* were under the control of a doctor, the *medicus ordinarius*. Although there has been considerable dispute about the precise role and status of the *medicus ordinarius* it seems most likely that this individual was a doctor with the rank of centurion.

A tombstone was found at Housesteads on Hadrian's Wall in the early nineteenth century. It was inscribed: 'To the spirits of the departed (and)

D M

A N I C I O

I N G E N V O

M E D I C O

O R D . C O H

I T V N G R

V I X . A N X X V

Diis Manibus

Anicio

Ingenuo

Medico

Ordinario (?) Cohortis

Primæ Tungrorum

Vixit annos viginti quinque

Size, 5 ft. by 2 ft. 6 in.

4. The remarkably embellished tombstone of the twenty-five-year-old *medicus ordinarius* Anicius Ingenuus, found at Housesteads on Hadrian's Wall.

to Anicius Ingenuus, *medicus ordinarius* of the First Cohort of Tungrians: he lived 25 years' (figure 4). The memorial was decorated with the relief of a hare crouching on a plinth under an arched wreath containing a central flower. Each of the upper corners is filled with a carefully carved roundel or rosette. Such embellishment is unusual, perhaps indicating the status of the individual among his fellow soldiers. The name Ingenuus means freeborn and it has been suggested that Anicius may have been the son of a Greek freedman.

At Caerleon in South Wales a bronze spatula has been discovered inscribed in fine punctated dots: 'C. CV... ANILI'. It was, perhaps, used for handling or applying ointments and has been translated: 'the property of CV's [? Cuspius or Curtius] century in charge of Manilianus'. It may be that Manilianus was the *medicus ordinarius* to this century of the Second Legion (figure 5).

One of the Vindolanda writing tablets indicates that thirty builders had been required to build a guest-house for Marcus the *medicus*. Another

5. A bronze spatula, probably for applying ointments, belonging to Manilianus, perhaps a *medicus ordinarius*, and found at Caerleon, Monmouthshire.

6. A collyrium stamp found at Kenchester (Herefordshire) inscribed in retrograde with the name 'Titus Vindacius Ariovistus' and the word '*chloron*', translated as 'green salve'. (Photograph: © The Trustees of The British Museum)

document refers to the presence of a *valetudinarium* or hospital. As will be discussed in chapter 5, there is evidence for military hospitals at a number of Roman forts and these would have required staffing. The running of the hospital was probably delegated to a junior officer, the *optio valetudinarii*.

Oculists

Oculist or collyrium stamps are found throughout the Western Roman Empire and over two dozen have been discovered in Britain. They were probably used for impressing the name of the maker or makers and the purposes of the treatment on to a hardened block of eye medication (collyrium).

The stamps are usually made of greenish schist or steatite and consist of small thin square blocks, generally with an inscription on each of the four edges (figure 6). In a few instances the stone is oblong with two inscribed sides, and in one example from Wroxeter the stamp is circular (figure 7). The letters are cut in intaglio form and written from right to left so that when stamped on the collyrium they make an impression that reads from left to right. The medications referred to on the stamps are discussed in chapter 4.

Epigraphic errors, as well as the occurrence of typically Celtic names such as Titus Vindacius Ariovistus and Gaius Silvius Tetricus, give credence to the local nature of the stamps. Nutton has suggested that the sticks

7. A collyrium stamp from Wroxeter in Shropshire (illustrated as it would appear on a collyrium), translated: 'Tiberius Claudius M...'s frankincense salve for every defect of the eyes: [to be used] with egg.'

of medicament were prepared in bulk at a central location for use by peripatetic doctors who made regular circuits round the Romano-British countryside. This might explain the four stamps from Colchester as well as the finds at rural sites such as the Wilcote villa in Oxfordshire. By analogy, at Avenches in Switzerland a *collegium* of doctors and teachers is referred to on a stone inscription set up by two *medici*, Q. Postumius Hyginus and Postumius Hermes. Interestingly, a collyrium stamp found 50 kilometres away at Vidy also mentions Postumius Hermes.

Two of the British collyrium stamps bear dual inscriptions, perhaps indicating that they may have been handed on from person to person or even down the generations. On an example from St Albans the name Flavius Secundus is executed in a rougher style than that of Lucius Julius Ivenis, suggesting a succession of ownership. The stamp from Biggleswade bears the names Gaius Valerius Amandus and Gaius Valerius Valentinus. They might have been father and son, or brothers, or freedmen of the same owner. Intriguingly, the grave of a doctor at Rheims in France contained, together with a collection of surgical instruments, the remains of three stamps. One was blank, the second bore the name Marcellinus and the third was inscribed with the name Gaius Firmius Severus.

List of inscribed collyrium stamps from Roman Britain

Location of find; present location; name on stamp
Bath, Somerset; now lost; Titus Junianus
Bath, Somerset; now lost; Flavius Litugnus or Litugenus
Biggleswade, Bedfordshire; British Museum; Gaius Valerius Amandus, Gaius Valerius Valentinus
Caistor-by-Norwich, Norfolk; British Museum; Publius Anicius Sedatus
Cambridge; Cambridge University Museum of Archaeology; Lucius Julius Salutaris, Marinus
Chester, Cheshire; Grosvenor Museum; Quintus Julius Martinus
Cirencester, Gloucestershire; British Museum; Minervalis
Cirencester, Gloucestershire; Corinium Museum; Atticus
Colchester, Essex; now lost; Quintus Julius Murranus
Colchester, Essex; British Museum; Lucius Ulpius Deciminus
Colchester, Essex; Colchester Castle Museum; Martialis
Colchester, Essex; Colchester Castle Museum; Publius Claudius Primus (? possible)
Dorchester, Dorset; Dorchester Museum; none
Harrold, Bedfordshire; Bedford Museum; Gaius Junius Tertullus
Ipswich, Suffolk; Ipswich Museum; none
Kenchester, Herefordshire; British Museum; Titus Vindacius Ariovistus
Kenchester, Herefordshire; Hereford Museum; Aurelius Polychronius
Leicester; now lost; Gaius Pal… Gracilis
Littleborough, Nottinghamshire; now lost; Julius Titianus (? possible)

London; Museum of London; Gaius Silvius Tetricus
Lydney, Gloucestershire; Lydney Park Museum; Julius Jucundus
St Albans, Hertfordshire; British Museum; Lucius Julius Ivenis, Flavius
 Secundus
Staines, Surrey; Surrey Archaeology Unit; Senior
Watercrook, Cumbria; Kendal Museum; P Clodianus
Wilcote, Oxfordshire; Ashmolean Museum; Maurus
Wroxeter, Shropshire; Shrewsbury Museum; Tiberius Claudius M…
Wroxeter, Shropshire; Shrewsbury Museum; Q… Lucillianus
York; Yorkshire Museum; Julius Alexander

Other healers

A range of other healers would also have probably been accessible to
the Romano-British patient. In addition to doctors, Galen lists trainers,
pharmacists, rootcutters, schoolmasters, eunuchs, boxers and grooms as
having roles in health care. A fragment of a stylus writing tablet found
in a first-century military ditch at Carlisle refers to '*Albino seplasario*'
(Albinus the pharmacist). One of the Vindolanda writing tablets also
mentions another pharmacist, Vitalis.

Medicine and religion were closely intertwined and, as will be discussed
in the next chapter, religious healing cults and personnel were present at
a number of sites in Roman Britain such as Bath and Lydney.

3
Religion and health

Religion was closely intertwined with all aspects of Roman life. Apollo was the original classical deity associated with medicine but, as time passed, Aesculapius, the son of Apollo by Coronis, gradually became the god more clearly linked with health care. Aesculapius was born by Caesarean section and trained in medicine by the centaur Chiron. The young Aesculapius is also said to have been guarded by serpents and dogs – two animals that subsequently became associated with the Aesculapian cult. The offspring of Aesculapius included Acesis (Telesphorus), Hygeia (Salus) and Panacea.

Although Aesculapius and his family were associated with health, it would be wrong to assume that healing was dissociated from the other ancient gods. Healing prayers or health-seeking offerings could be directed to any god according to the individual's preference. The Romans were also not rigid in their name for the goddess of health, with Minerva Medica (the equivalent of the Greek Athena) sometimes being substituted for Salus.

As well as the ubiquitous Aesculapius and Apollo, localised modifications of their cults can be identified within Roman Britain, and there is also evidence for specific local healing centres.

Aesculapius in Britain

Aesculapius was associated with specific terrestrial locations and resided in his temple. The three most famous Greek temples were located at Epidaurus, Cos and Pergamum, while the first Roman temple to Aesculapius was built on Tiber Island. According to legend, Aesculapius arrived on the island in the form of a snake, having been invited across from Epidaurus to deal with a plague that was afflicting Rome in the third century BC.

Water was a central element of the Aesculapian religious practices and it was drunk for its healing properties as well as being used for bathing and ritual cleansing. When an individual had been purified by the sacred waters he or she was taken to an *abaton*, a special dormitory, in order to experience ritual temple sleep. During this 'incubation' phase Aesculapius was said to appear in a dream-vision and either heal the individual directly or provide him with guidance about what was required to effect a cure. However, sometimes the instructions given to the individual in the context of the dream were so cryptic that they required clarification by a member of the temple staff, the interpreter of dreams.

The incubation process also involved priests and priestesses circulating among the sleepers with serpents and dogs, the curative dreams being augmented by the touches of the priests or the links of dogs and serpents. Numismatic evidence suggests that the Aesculapian serpent was the species *Elaphe longissima* and that the sacred dog resembled a hunting dog similar to an Irish wolfhound.

The Aesculapian cult was popularised by Greek physicians moving throughout the empire. The Greek inscriptions at Chester and Binchester referred to earlier (figures 1, 2 and 3), as well as other examples from Maryport (Cumbria) and Carlisle, were probably all left by Greek doctors. Furthermore, an elaborately carved altar dedicated to Fortuna, Aesculapius and Salus by the household staff of the imperial legate has also been discovered at Chester. On the left side of the stone is a ladle crossed with the rod of Aesculapius, around which a serpent twines; below are two flesh-hooks and a sacrificial knife.

Although no temples to Aesculapius have yet been discovered in Britain, several altars have come to light, as have a statuette of Aesculapius from Chichester (Sussex) and an intaglio from Braintree (Essex, figure 8). Some of the inscriptions also show an interesting transition from the Greek to the Latin: the altar found at Lancaster is inscribed in both languages and the one from Tunstall (Lancashire) uses Latin script but Greek terms. A probable statue of Telesphorus has also been found at the Hadrian's Wall fort of Birdoswald.

Aesculapius was a favourite subject on the coinage of the middle Roman Imperial period from the second and third centuries AD. Furthermore, both Septimus Severus and Caracalla, who visited Britain,

8. An intaglio found at Braintree (Essex), perhaps from a ring belonging to a doctor, depicting Aesculapius and Hygeia (Salus). The letters 'APE' cut in retrograde might possibly be an allusion to the Hippocratic oath. (Photograph: Mark Hassall)

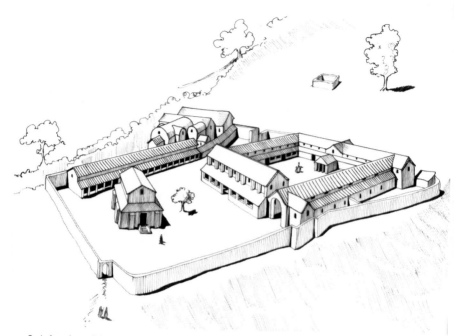

9. A drawing of the temple complex at Lydney (Gloucestershire) as it might have appeared in the fourth century AD. The temple stands alone in front of a long narrow building, the *abaton*. To the right of the temple is the guest-house and at the rear of the complex is the bath-house. (© Guy de la Bédoyère)

had Aesculapian representations on both their local coinages and on the standard issue *denarius*, perhaps illustrating their personal interest in the cult and its spread. Indeed, Caracalla had sought treatment for his various ailments at the Aesculapian shrine in Pergamum. Both Clodius Albinus, a governor of Britain with imperial ambitions, and Carausius, the so-called British usurper, minted coins in Britain depicting Aesculapius.

Local modifications: Lydney

Despite the lack of evidence for any Aesculapian sanctuary in Britain, it has been suggested that the Celtic god Nodens was a healing deity in Aesculapian style. The temple complex at Lydney in Gloucestershire shares many features with the major Aesculapian temples. Like a number of ritual healing sites, the location is impressive, being sited on the top of a small hill with views across the River Severn.

As can be seen from the drawing, the religious complex was extensive (figure 9). The temple itself was constructed with a central raised *cella* surrounded by an ambulatory or processional corridor. Projecting off this were several bays or chapels that may still be clearly seen today, as can the steps leading into the main entrance of the temple at the south-east (figures 10 and 11). In the nineteenth century a mosaic was uncovered within the

10. The steps leading up into the entrance of the temple of Nodens at Lydney.

11. The remains of the processional corridor surrounding the temple of Nodens, looking across to the raised *cella* in the middle of the building.

12. The remains of the bath-house associated with the temple complex of Nodens at Lydney.

cella decorated with fishes and sea monsters and inscribed: 'D M N T FLAVIUS SENILIS PR REL EX STIPIBUS POSSUIT O[PITU]LANTE VICTORINO INTERP[RE]TIANTE.' This has been translated: 'For the god Mars Nodens, Titus Flavius Senilis, superintendent of the cult, from the offerings had this laid; Victorinus, the interpreter (of dreams), gave his assistance.'

Near to the temple stood three contemporary buildings: a square courtyard house, a well-equipped suite of baths (figure 12), and a long narrow building containing many cubicles. Further to the north, a large water tank supplied the baths and the guest-house. It has been suggested that the long building might have been used as the *abaton* and that the large house could have served to accommodate the visiting worshippers.

Many items traditionally associated with healing cults have been found at Lydney. In addition to over eight thousand coins, 320 pins and 300 bracelets and brooches have been unearthed, perhaps gifts from

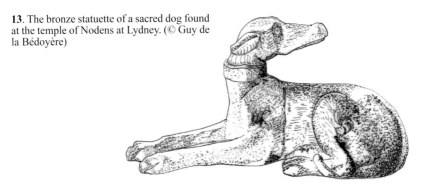

13. The bronze statuette of a sacred dog found at the temple of Nodens at Lydney. (© Guy de la Bédoyère)

women relieved of labour problems. There were also four inscriptions to the deity: two to Nodens equated with Mars, and two to Nodens alone. Unlike at the Greek Aesculapian temples, no representations of serpents (*Elaphe longissima*) were found at Lydney, but rather nine statuettes of dogs in stone or bronze (figure 13). Perhaps such 'healing'

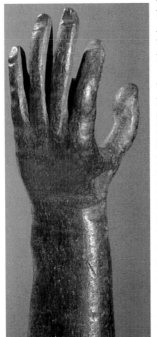

dogs were more appropriate to Britain than the non-native 'healing' *Elaphe longissima*. Another medically related find from Lydney was a slate collyrium stamp inscribed with the name Julius Jucundus.

As discussed in the introduction, anatomical votives were a special form of gift given to the ancient gods either in the hope of a cure or as a thank-offering. When an individual had undertaken to give a particular payment in return for a service rendered, the gift is usually referred to as an ex-voto. Anatomical votives depicting diseased areas of the body have been found at many ancient healing shrines; some were clearly mass-produced and generally illustrate normal anatomy whereas others seem to represent specific diseases. At Lydney a votive female figure, a votive leg and foot and a votive forearm have been unearthed.

14. The votive forearm with spoon-shaped nails (*koilonychia*), from the temple of Nodens at Lydney. (Photograph: Dr G. Hart)

Detailed examination of the votive forearm (figure 14) reveals that the nails of the hand are spoon-shaped. This is referred to as *koilonychia* and is a well-recognised physical sign of iron-deficiency anaemia; perhaps this was the condition for which the patient was seeking help. Interestingly, Dwarf Hill, on which the temple stands, consists of red ferrous limestone and the water used at Lydney would have been particularly rich in iron.

Local modifications: Bath

The development of the cult of Sulis Minerva at Bath may have been based on a local deity adopted by the Romans. As the many altars and tombstones illustrate, the spa and temple complex attracted pilgrims and other individuals, both military and civilian, from Britain and elsewhere. The site appears to have been occupied from the reign of Nero until the late fourth century.

Aside from the association of the temple of Sulis Minerva with the baths and the hot springs (figures 15 and 16), the evidence for a healing cult is supported by the finding of two examples of bronze and ivory breast votives. Bath has also produced two collyrium stamps in the names of Titus Junianus and Flavius Litugnus (or Litugenus).

15. A view of the Great Bath at Bath. The Roman masonry survives to a height of 1–2 metres.

16. The hot spring water enters the bathing complex at Bath at a temperature of 49°C and flows at a rate of a third of a million gallons per day.

A relief of a man, woman, dog, snake and tree found at the Cross Street Bath site near the temple of Sulis Minerva suggests an Aesculapian-like healing centre but, because of the extensive urban development since Roman times, it has not yet been possible to find footprints of any typical cult buildings. However, it can be tentatively suggested that the circular temple (*tholos*) and the building decorated with the façade of the four seasons might have been integral parts of an Aesculapian-type cult. At the Aesculapian temple at Epidaurus the underground labyrinth associated with the *tholos* was probably a snake pit. Cunliffe has also suggested that the façade of the four seasons might have decorated an *abaton*.

A further intriguing find from Bath is an inscription recording a gift, probably a statue, erected for the goddess Sulis Minerva by the haruspex Lucius Marcius Memor. As described in chapter 1, the Romans inherited some of their ideas about medicine from the Etruscans, including haruspication.

Other local healing deities

At Carrawburgh on Hadrian's Wall excavations have revealed a

Romano-Celtic temple. The associated well yielded twenty-four altars: ten specifically dedicated to Coventina and one to Minerva. On the latter, Minerva is portrayed standing on the right of a mutilated Aesculapius, but with the serpent still clearly visible between them. Another damaged stone representation of Aesculapius has been found at the nearby fort of Chesters. The other significant finds in support of a healing cult at Carrawburgh consist of a stone head, several small bronze heads, bronze models of a horse and a dog, a life-sized bronze hand and more than thirteen thousand coins.

Elsewhere in Britain possible healing cults have been identified that are unrelated to baths, springs or wells. At Muntham Court near Findon in Sussex there is a circular shrine of Roman date. Finds of a pommel (perhaps from a mace), a plaque depicting a crouching bear, ox skulls and a clay model of a leg demonstrate the site's sacred character. The leg is similar, albeit of coarser material, to the votive bronzes from Lydney and Carrawburgh. A bronze votive leg has also been found at the shrine of Mercury at Uley in Gloucestershire; it depicts the congenital condition of *genu recurvatum* or back knee.

Outside the walls of Caerwent Roman city in Monmouthshire a Romano-Celtic shrine with an associated long building has been excavated. Here the discovery of skulls, a bone bird and a bronze snake suggest a healing cult. Close to the temple were also found some probable ritual pits; one contained human and ox skulls and two had the skulls of five dogs.

As evidenced by the findings of collyrium stamps at Lydney and Bath, in addition to the Aesculapian dedications by doctors, it may be an artificial division to separate rigidly the spiritual from the physical aspects of Romano-British health care. There may have been a particular focus on eye care at Wroxeter, where two collyrium stamps in the names of

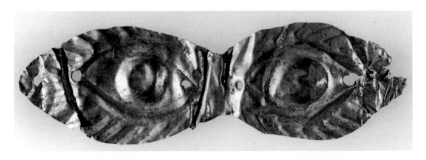

17. A pair of votive sheet-gold eyes unearthed at Wroxeter (Shropshire) in the north-west corner of the baths-basilica. (Photograph: © The Trustees of The British Museum)

18. Roughly made models of eyes cut from plaster and found at Wroxeter. (Photograph: ©
English Heritage)

Tiberius Claudius and Q... Lucillianus were discovered, together with a
case of probable surgical instruments, including an eye needle for cataract
extraction (see chapter 5). However, this evidence of 'physical medicine'
is complemented by the presence at Wroxeter of eye votives. In 1967 a
piece of sheet gold in the shape of a pair of eyes (figure 17) was found
at the north-west corner of the baths-basilica. In the same area bronze
eyes have been unearthed in addition to numerous eyes carved from wall
plaster (figure 18). Wroxeter has also yielded an altar to Apollo, who was
considered to have a particular association with eyes.

4
Diseases and treatments

The evidence for specific diseases in the Romano-British population depends on the conditions affecting the surviving human remains. The commonest archaeological findings are skeletal but even these are highly dependent on the environment and burial practices.

In the human remains excavated at Cirencester the proportion of bones showing evidence of fractures was high. In comparison with Bronze Age material from Britain, injuries were particularly common around the ankle. This perhaps reflects the shift towards increasing levels of agriculture, for walking across ploughed fields would have predisposed the Romano-British farmer to twisting injuries and ankle fractures. Further evidence for heavy labouring tasks comes from an analysis of spinal columns.

At York, a *colonia* for retired soldiers, a wealth of skeletal material was excavated from the Roman cemetery at Trentholme Drive. In particular there was evidence of twenty-one healed fractures of the upper and lower limbs including fractured thigh bones, possibly as a result of battle injuries. Several other thigh bones were also noted to have depressions consistent with sword cuts. In one example of a virtually complete skeleton, the man had sustained several fractured ribs together with a dent in his thigh bone associated with a bony outgrowth – perhaps a secondary bone reaction to injury. In another case the healed fractures seem likely to have been associated with an open wound as there was fusion of the bones around the elbow (humerus, ulna and radius) probably related to an associated bone infection.

The average heights of men and women based on skeletal remains from York were 1.69 metres and 1.59 metres respectively. These figures are comparable to the modern British population, implying that the residents of York had been reasonably well nourished. More specifically, there was no evidence of scurvy (vitamin C deficiency) or osteomalacia (vitamin D deficiency) in any of the bones examined.

Analysis of the content of the Roman diet based on finds of vegetable and animal matter at various sites in Britain suggests that it was well balanced and high in fibre. Beans, lentils, figs, hazelnuts, dates and a variety of fruits have been discovered at many Roman sites. Excavations at Brough-on-Noe (Derbyshire) have also uncovered the remains of an amphora that had contained plums from Spain; it was inscribed 'PRVN.. A'. Thus it seems likely that the Romans were troubled less by the 'low dietary fibre' diseases such as cancer of the large bowel that cause such problems today.

Possibly due to increased sugar consumption during the Roman period from sweetened wine, imported dates and the use of honey, dental problems were very prevalent among the Romano-Britons. During the Iron Age dental disease affected 7.5 per cent of the population but this rose to 11.3 per cent after the Roman occupation. In addition to caries, there was a parallel increase in the extent of tooth loss and evidence of dental abscesses. A pair of iron dental forceps with a copper alloy pivot has been found at Kirkby Thore (Cumbria), suggesting the presence of dental care.

Another disease that seems likely to have been relatively common in the Roman world compared with today was lead poisoning. In children this can lead to learning difficulties, behavioural problems, stunted growth, anaemia and kidney damage. In adults the consequences range from infertility to muscle, nerve and joint disorders. Possible sources of lead in Roman Britain included water piping (figure 19), cooking vessels, imported wine and even some medical treatments.

In the early Republic the Romans had discovered the mechanism of sweetening and preserving sour wines with lead-containing additives. They found that *sapa*, a syrup prepared by concentrating must in a lead

19. A length of lead piping still *in situ* adjacent to the Great Bath at Bath.

vessel, kept wine from spoiling and gave it an agreeable flavour. Based on Roman descriptions for preserving wine in this fashion, Eisinger repeated the process. He found that the ingestion of such lead-preserved wine would provide an individual with a dose of 20 mg of lead per litre of wine drunk. The chronic toxicity limit above which symptoms of lead poisoning will occur is one fortieth of this.

Some circumstantial evidence for lead poisoning comes from the finding of severe gout in an individual interred within a high-status stone sarcophagus found at Cirencester. Moreover, hair analysis from a similar burial at Dorchester (Dorset) revealed twenty-five times more lead in the Roman samples in comparison with modern samples. It is unlikely that the raised lead concentration in the hair is simply a contaminant from cosmetics or the lead coffin lining as further analyses have demonstrated even higher levels of lead in the skull. Furthermore, other work has examined the lead in tooth enamel and found that concentrations increased by a hundredfold during the Romano-British period.

Among the Romano-British burials at both Cirencester and Dorchester were large numbers of bones with thickened marrow cavities and other bony changes usually associated with iron-deficiency anaemia. Possible causes for such anaemia include dietary deficiencies, poor intake of iron through the gut wall (e.g. due to parasites such as those identified in the Roman sewers at York), blood loss and lead poisoning. As mentioned in the previous chapter, at the Aesculapian-like temple of Nodens in Lydney a small votive bronze arm and hand was identified with spoon-shaped nails (figure 14), and iron deficiency is one possible cause of such deformity.

According to Celsus, dietetics, pharmacology and surgery were the three branches into which medical treatments could be categorised. However, there was always some blurring of the boundaries between these, as dietetics often included such treatments as bathing and exercise in addition to the regulation of food and drink. In relation to pharmacology, numerous herbs, spices, vegetables and minerals were used as treatments.

In the late sixteenth century, the antiquary William Camden visited Hadrian's Wall and wrote: 'the Roman souldiers of the marches did plant heere every where in old time for their use, certain medicinable hearbes, for to cure wounds: whence it is that some Emperick practitioners of Chirurgery in Scotland, flock hither every yeere in the beginning of summer, to gather such simples and wound herbes; the vertue whereof they highly commend as found by long experience, and to be of singular efficacy.'

The remains of a number of specific plants that could have had a role in medical treatment have been identified from Roman Britain. Examples include celery, poppy seeds, henbane, rue, cabbage and dock. However, although all these were promoted as therapies by Roman medical authors, such bio-archaeological finds need to be treated with great caution. Although cabbage (found at Vindolanda) was recommended as both a laxative and as a poultice there is simply no evidence that the remains identified actually served either of those purposes. The faecal remains in the sewers at Bearsden on the Antonine Wall in Scotland contained seeds of celery (used to improve urine output) and opium poppy but, again, this indicates only that the substances were ingested, not *why* they were ingested. Opium was used as a culinary flavouring as well as an analgesic.

If we accept that medication and dietary modifications were equally important approaches to treatment in Roman Britain, this adds another level of uncertainty to any organic finds. Thus, even if the imported figs found in London or Silchester (Hampshire) were 'medical', they might have been used to treat the patient by dietary modification rather than, as suggested by Celsus, cooked over charcoal and then specifically used for coughs and sore throats.

Associated with the finds of the remains of herbs at the hospital in the legionary fortress of Neuss in Germany were various implements for grinding them into powder for use in prescriptions. Pestles and mortars have also been identified in Britain, and so have instruments that may have been used for weighing drugs. Simple folding balances have been found at Chester and Lydney, and bronze steelyards have been unearthed at Wroxeter and Richborough (Kent). At Silchester finds of small bronze balance arms were associated with stone palettes of marble and greenstone, possibly for grinding medicines and rolling pills. In the museum at Chesters on Hadrian's Wall there is a triangular medicine weight of tin, as well as counterpoises, many in the form of snakes, and therefore, perhaps, for medical purposes.

Although wine might have caused disease either by means of the lead or the ethanol it contained, there is evidence that wine was also used as a vehicle for medication and that such medicated wine was widely exported. According to Dioscorides, Celsus and Pliny, horehound was frequently used to treat chest complaints and a shard of an amphora inscribed *prasi[on]* (horehound) in Greek letters has been discovered at Carpow in Scotland. The Aminean wine that found its way to Caerleon in an amphora marked 'AMINE' might also have been used as a treatment for diarrhoea if taken with wheat or bread.

Treatments based on copper, lead, zinc, iron and arsenic are frequently encountered in the various Roman treatment lists. For example, realgar, the orange-red crystalline disulphate of arsenic, was recommended by Celsus as an antiseptic for the cleansing of wounds and ulcerations. In

1895 excavators at Silchester found some tiny lumps of realgar; this was originally considered to have come from an artist's palette but it might equally have been contained within a doctor's medicine box.

As mentioned in chapter 2, a number of collyrium stamps have been found in Britain. The example from Cambridge is inscribed on one face 'L. IVL. SALVTARIS PE/NICILLUM AD LIPPITUD' ('the collyrium of Lucius Julius Salutaris, to be applied with a fine brush for *lippitudo* of the eyes'), and on a second side 'MARINI CAES' ('the collyrium named *caesarianum* according to the recipe of Marinus'). *Caesarianum* was known to Celsus, who indicated that it could be used for *lippitudo* and consisted of shoemaker's blacking, *misy* (?copper pyrites), white pepper, poppy-tears (opium), gum, zinc oxide and antimony sulphide. The term *lippitudo* probably covered a range of eye problems such as

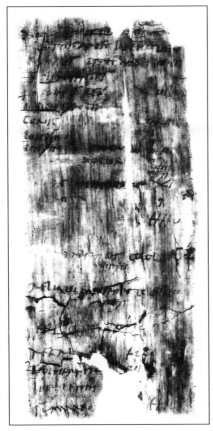

20. A writing tablet from Vindolanda reporting the strength of the First Cohort of Tungrians. One third were unfit with eye problems – *lippientes*. (© The Vindolanda Trust)

conjunctivitis and other inflammatory or infectious conditions.

Poppy ointments and salves for *lippitudo* are referred to on the stamps from London (Gaius Silvius Tetricus) and Biggleswade (Gaius Valerius Valentinus) and, in total, eleven of the collyrium stamps found in the United Kingdom to date refer to the condition. Furthermore, the strength report of the First Cohort of Tungrians found at Vindolanda (figure 20) declares that thirty-one individuals were unfit and, of these, a third had *lippientes*. The text, with translation, is given as: *aegri xv* (sick 15), *volnerati vi* (wounded 6), *lippientes x* (eye trouble 10). A leather eye patch has also been found at Vindolanda.

Galen mentions 124 pathological conditions of the eyes but it is not easy to match these and the terms on the collyrium stamps to the problems we recognise today. *Ad claritatem* might refer to short-sightedness, which would now be resolved by using spectacles. Gaius Valerius Valentinus' mixture (Biggleswade stamp) and Quintus Julius Murranus' quince ointment (Colchester stamp) were both designed for 'clearing the vision'. Furthermore, the Colchester stamp also refers to a balsam salve for blurred vision and the Biggleswade stamp to a salve for dim sight. It has been suggested that these preparations worked (albeit transiently) by their astringent actions.

Ad reumatica (running eyes), *cicatrices* (scars), *sicca* (swellings) and *aspritudo* appear on a number of stamps. Six of the collyrium stamps from Britain refer to *aspritudo* and this condition may simply relate to the problems arising from untreated or chronic conjunctivitis. Certainly Celsus remarks that *aspritudo* would readily develop in eyes already made sore by other means.

A large number of the eye remedies contained antiseptics in one form or another. The vinegar lotion of Gaius Valerius Amandus (Biggleswade stamp) or the copper oxide of Aurelius Polychronius (Kenchester stamp) would have been very effective antiseptics either in treating conjunctivitis or in preventing any scar on the eye becoming infected while it healed. The salve of the British oculist Axius referred to by Galen also had many antiseptic components in terms of its metallic content: 'Mercuric sulphide eye salve of Axius, oculist of the British fleet, for ulcerated corners of the eye, bad inflammation of the eye, intense irritation and chronic condition. Copper and zinc oxide 96 grams, zinc carbonate 96 grams, saffron 64 grams, mercuric sulphide 64 grams, opium 48 grams, acacia 96 grams, rainwater as much as is necessary.'

5
Surgery, medical instruments and hospitals

A large number of surgical procedures are described by the Roman medical authors. These ranged from amputations to open abdominal surgery, the suturing of small lacerations and even cataract operations. Furthermore, many instruments described as 'surgical' or 'medical' have been identified from sites in Britain by making a comparison with descriptions contained within the classical medical texts. However, although we might have a view about the role of a particular instrument in relation to both modern and ancient surgical practice, whether the object really served that purpose is often debatable.

Today's doctors perform a different range of operations from their Roman predecessors, using some dissimilar surgical techniques. Moreover, the wounds sustained during battle in the ancient world would have been quite distinct from those encountered in modern warfare and obviously required different approaches. The absence of effective anaesthesia would have also been an important consideration for the Roman surgeon.

Operations on the uvula (the fleshy tag hanging down at the back of the throat) were common in Roman times, because of concerns about the adverse effects of an inflamed uvula, but are very rare today. Three sets of uvula forceps (or *staphylagra*) have been unearthed in Britain and, as can be seen from the illustration of the Caerwent example, the branches of the forceps are crossed and pivot around a rivet joint like a pair of scissors (figure 21). This instrument is 19.4 cm long and the

21. A pair of uvula forceps (*staphylagra*) found at Caerwent (Monmouthshire). Operations on the uvula were common in Roman times but are rare today. (Photograph: Newport Museum)

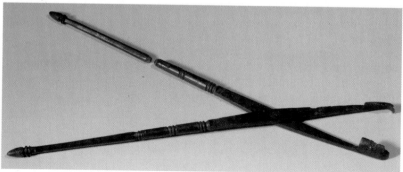

jaws, which project forward enclosing a cup for the amputated uvula, bear fine teeth. The teeth were probably used to crush the neck of the uvula, thereby reducing the chances of haemorrhage, which was quite a problem if the uvula was simply cut.

As mentioned in the introduction, Roman medicine was based on theories and ideas different from those of modern medical practice. Thus some of the surgical procedures described by Roman authors would perhaps be labelled cosmetic today. The Romans considered shaving and cutting the hair as an important surgical approach to treating several diseases, and the culter found at Sandy in Bedfordshire could thus be considered a potential surgical tool as well as a simple razor.

A set of medical instruments dating from the AD 50s was found buried in a grave at Stanway near Colchester. The more typical surgical instruments (i.e. scalpels, hooks, forceps, needles and a saw) were accompanied by some other finds, including eight possible divination rods. It has been suggested that they were cast on the ground and the resulting distribution read, perhaps for diagnostic or prognostic purposes. If the rods were an integral component of a patient's medical care, then they also should probably be considered as 'medical' instruments.

One of the major problems of any modern classification of medical/ surgical instruments is that it does not allow for the generic nature of many instruments. Hammers and chisels were used in bone surgery, but also by blacksmiths and carpenters (and occasionally by other healers to make splints for fractures). A number of clearly identified surgical instruments have been discovered at Wroxeter but whether the Roman lead hammer found there was surgical or otherwise can only be guessed at. Even today, many of the instruments found in an orthopaedic surgeon's instrument tray would not be out of place in a cabinet maker's workshop – e.g. saws, bone levers, bone forceps and drills. Celsus highlights this issue in his description of the replacement of a bone in the case of a compound fracture: 'when a small fragment of bone projects... it is pushed back into place... and if this cannot be done with the hand, pincers, such as smiths use, must be applied... [and] force the projecting bone into place' (Celsus VIII, 60). The blacksmith's tongs found at Tremadoc in North Wales are most likely the type recommended by Celsus and might also have been 'surgical'.

To complicate matters further, there is also evidence of treatment variations across the Roman Empire. Celsus stated (*Prooemium* 30) that 'methods of practice differ according to the nature of localities, and that one method is required in Rome, another in Egypt, another in Gaul'. Thus certain tools may have been applied in a different fashion in Roman Britain to elsewhere in the empire, and it is possible that some medical instruments being used in the provinces did not even warrant a mention

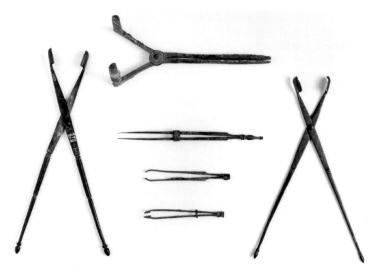

22. A selection of Roman medical instruments from the British Museum, including a variety of types of forceps. (Photograph: © The Trustees of The British Museum)

in the elite Roman texts. It has also been suggested that in the more peripheral regions of the Roman Empire a potential surgical instrument may have been used for more than one purpose. For example, scalpels were important tools for leatherworking in addition to surgery, preparing medicines or cutting bandages. *Staphylagra* might have been used to treat

23. A selection of Roman surgical instruments from the British Museum, including a number of scalpel handles. (Photograph: © The Trustees of The British Museum)

haemorrhoids in addition to problems relating to the uvula.

A large number of potential surgical instruments have been found across the Roman Empire (figures 22 and 23). The majority of surviving examples from Britain are of iron or bronze and it seems possible that the more common surgical instruments were made locally. There is evidence of metalworking in many Romano-British towns, and extensive ironworking occurred in specific areas such as the Forest of Dean. It is also likely that some instruments were made out of tin since Britain was a major source of this metal for the rest of the Roman Empire. Hippocrates mentions uterine sounds (used to procure abortions) made of tin but, unfortunately, time is not kind to tin and the only surviving example from Britain of a possible medical object of tin is a weight in the museum at Chesters.

Forceps had a key place in Roman surgery; they could be used for holding tissues, removing splints or eyelashes. However, the problem is that the removal of body hair was also a feature of Romanisation behaviour as a hairless body was perceived as the Roman ideal. It has often been difficult to determine whether forceps had surgical or cosmetic/social roles but it is now generally agreed that forceps greater than 8 cm long and of better craftsmanship were more likely to have had a surgical function.

The Littleborough forceps (figure 24) was made in one piece from a cast copper alloy, probably brass. It is 15.5 cm long and consists of two elements: the forceps itself and a crook-shaped hook. In common with a similar type of surgical forceps found at Silchester it seems likely that a metal slider linked the arms together. The jaws of the forceps are 17 mm wide and on each of the edges teeth had been carefully cut so that the two jaws interlocked exactly. Of particular interest, and by analogy with an identical example from Trier in Germany, it has been suggested

24. The set of brass surgical forceps found at Littleborough (Nottinghamshire) and probably used for holding tissues. (Drawings by Siân Summerton)

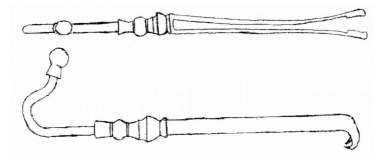

that the tip of the hook was stylised as a snake's head.

Jackson emphasises the importance of context in assigning a surgical role to an instrument that could have had a variety of uses. Although nothing akin to the finds preserved by the disasters at Pompeii (volcanic eruption) or Rimini (fire) discussed in the introduction has been uncovered in Britain, possible contextual finds have been identified at Wroxeter, Corbridge and Caerleon in addition to the Stanway burial referred to earlier.

In 1862, excavations at Wroxeter uncovered a grave in which was found, among other likely medical objects, a possible surgeon's lancet. According to Wright, this lancet had been in a box in which were also found some beads of coloured and striped glass, a piece of a needle or bodkin and the remains of two very small earthen vessels containing a very hard substance resembling white paint. He considered that he had discovered a doctor's box in the grave of a Roman surgeon. Based on a contemporary drawing of the lancet, it has been suggested that the lancet might have been used for venesection or the drainage of abscesses and fluid-filled body cavities (figure 25).

Corbridge fort has also produced a significant quantity of probable medical instruments. The collection included knives, forceps and needles, together with a large number and variety of probes. Spatulate probes with an olivary tip at one end and a flat spatula at the other were particularly common. These might have been used for investigating wounds as well

as mixing and applying medicines. However, they may also have had numerous non-medical functions such as mixing and applying cosmetics. Finding them in association with more established medical instruments is helpful in suggesting a medical purpose.

At Caerleon fort, plotting the find sites for possible surgical instruments suggests that they seem to be clustered with a particular concentration around the bath-house. Children's teeth showing signs of surgical extraction have been found in the associated drains leading from the bath-house, indicating that medical treatment would probably have occurred there.

Quality is also an issue to consider in assigning a surgical/medical role to a particular instrument. The lingula-probe from Silchester is of unusually good

25. A surgeon's lancet from a grave at Wroxeter. It was possibly used for the drainage of abscesses or for venesection.

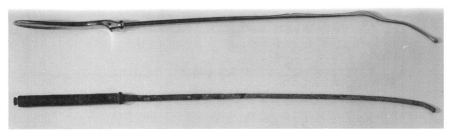

26. A uterine sound from Hockwold (Norfolk), compared with a modern example (above). Such uterine sounds might have been used to procure abortions in Roman Britain. (Photograph: Norwich Museum)

quality with a stem inlaid with silver wire. The possible uterine sound from Hockwold (Norfolk) bears a remarkable resemblance to a modern example (figure 26).

In demonstrating any surgical practice in Roman Britain it is important to appreciate that very few operations will leave any tangible palaeopathological evidence in terms of the effects on any surviving human remains. Furthermore, an undisplaced fracture will heal in exactly the same way as will a fracture in which bone forceps or bone elevators had been used to reposition the displaced bones. The pathologist examining the remains two thousand years later is thus unable to state whether any surgical instruments were used in the treatment of the fracture.

Trephination, during which a hole was made in a person's skull, was described by Celsus as a treatment for head wounds. At least three examples of possible trephination have been found in Britain: at Whitchurch, Trentholme Drive (York) and Cirencester. In the last example it seems that the skull might have been pressing on the brain, perhaps inducing fits. Moreover, the evidence of new bone growth around the area of the trephine suggests that the patient survived the surgery.

Cataract extraction was well described by Celsus: 'he is to be seated opposite the surgeon in a light room… the assistant from behind holds the head so that the patient does not move. Thereupon a needle is to be taken, pointed enough to penetrate, yet not too fine, and this is to be

27. A possible cataract needle found at Brading (Isle of Wight). The sharpened end may have been used to perform the surgery, and the terminal blob at the opposite end to cauterise the wound. (Photograph: Brading Roman Villa)

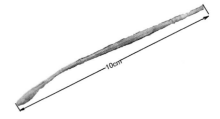

inserted straight through the two outer tunics. When the [correct] spot is reached, the needle is to be sloped... and should gently rotate there and little by little guide it [i.e. the lens with the cataract] below the region of the pupil' (Celsus VII, 7, 14).

By analogy with finds from Pompeii, possible cataract needles (*specilla*) have been found at Carlisle, Piddington (Northamptonshire) and Brading (Isle of Wight), although it is important to appreciate that such objects may be very similar in appearance to a broken scoop probe. The Brading example (figure 27) is sharpened at one end and angled with a blob at the other. Once the cataract had been displaced, the blob may have been heated and used for cauterising the wound. The Brading instrument was found in association with a bone token in the form of an eye-shaped lozenge with a central dot and ring representing the pupil. The room where both these items were discovered also contained a mosaic with a geometric pattern in the shape of a lozenge with a central circle, and it has tentatively been suggested that this room was specifically used to treat eye ailments. Similar eye tokens and *specilla* have also been found together at the water sanctuary of Pouillé in France and it is notable that a supply of spring water was also available at Brading associated with a water feature, possibly a water deity.

Hospitals (*valetudinaria*)

The existence of military hospitals at many Roman forts in Britain such as Inchtuthil, Caerleon, Chester, Housesteads, Benwell and Wallsend has been contentious. Much of the evidence is based on analogy with similar sites in Germany such as Neuss and Haltern, together with the writings of Caesar and Pseudo-Hyginus. From a description in *De Bello Gallico* it seems that Caesar's field hospitals consisted of a number of smaller tents arranged in an open square around a central marquee. Pseudo-Hyginus in his *Liber de Munitionibus Castrorum* was particularly concerned about the siting of the *valetudinarium* within the fort in order to allow the patients peace and quiet.

A fragmentary tablet from Vindolanda mentions the word *valetudinarium* and at Housesteads a possible hospital has been identified in a quiet location behind the *principia*. It follows the standard plan of a hospital with a series of small rooms arranged around a courtyard (see illustration on front cover). The building also had its own latrine in the south-west corner (figures 28 and 29) and, perhaps, a small plunge bath. The entrance was near the north end of the west wall and led into a probable reception room where patients might have been directed to the wards or straight into a possible operating theatre in the north range. Although no surgical instruments have been unearthed at the hospital site, the tombstone of Anicius Ingenuus referred to in chapter 2 and some probable surgical

28. A view of some of the small rooms surrounding the central courtyard within the hospital building (*valetudinarium*) at Housesteads on Hadrian's Wall.

29. The drain leading from the latrine within the hospital building (*valetudinarium*) at Housesteads.

hooks (used for seizing and holding the margins of wounds) have been found at Housesteads.

It has been estimated that there were ten wards at Housesteads with two or three beds per ward. Wallsend hospital might have accommodated eight to twelve patients at any one time. However, such figures allow for a casualty rate of only 2 to 3 per cent, suggesting that the *valetudinaria* were not designed for convalescence. Soldiers requiring long-term care might therefore have been granted sick leave to recuperate elsewhere: certainly a third of the Roman visitors at Bath were soldiers, including two centurions, a number of legionaries and a Spanish cavalryman.

6
Architecture and health

To the medical historian Rome is frequently held up as an example of excellence in public health. It is often stated that the Romans developed high-quality clean-water delivery systems in addition to efficient waste disposal. They are also credited with improving the housing stock and the domestic living conditions of the inhabitants of the Roman Empire.

The problem is that we often view ancient architectural innovations such as aqueducts, drains and bath-houses through modern eyes or by reference to the writings of an educated elite living in Rome. In *De Aquaeductu Urbis Romae* Sextus Julius Frontinus recognised that, as water commissioner, he had an important role in protecting the health of the citizens of Rome. However, whether he had adopted a similar perspective when he had previously been governor of Roman Britain is difficult to gauge.

Some structural developments may even have had a detrimental effect on the public health. For example, the excellent roads and improved communications would have contributed to the ease with which diseases were spread. In Britain the increased contacts with other areas of the empire following the invasion of AD 43, combined with the trend towards greater urbanisation, would have led to both the introduction and the spread of new diseases. There is certainly palaeopathological evidence for population-density dependent illnesses such as tuberculosis and leprosy first occurring in Britain during the Roman Period. Moreover, according to Roberts and Cox, the prevalence of non-specific infections identified from excavated skeletal remains rises from 1.5 per cent during the Iron Age to 6.7 per cent during the Roman period.

Water supply

Although Roman Britain cannot boast an equivalent of the Pont du Gard in Gaul, evidence for aqueducts and water distribution systems can be found at the sites of forts, *coloniae*, *civitas* capitals and many smaller Romano-British towns. However, most of these 'aqueducts' were actually little more than lined channels or single pipelines and it has been argued that few of them could have provided much water for domestic consumption. For example, the 'aqueduct' supplying the fort at Brough-on-Noe (Derbyshire) probably delivered about as much water as an average domestic tap does today. In places such as Bath or Chelmsford there would have been little water left over for domestic consumers after supplying the bath-house and the *mansio* (inn). Furthermore, although

30. The aqueduct pipeline at Lincoln consisted of a series of interlocking earthenware pipes encased in a waterproof concrete jacket. (Photograph: Michael Jones)

the majority of forts possessed aqueduct supplies, perhaps because of the ready availability of skilled military personnel such as surveyors and architects, some of this water may have been used for purposes other than human consumption. At Dolaucothi in Wales, for example, the aqueduct also supplied water for various industrial purposes associated with the gold mines.

At Lincoln the aqueduct consists of a series of interlocking earthenware pipes each nearly a metre long and with a maximum internal diameter of 14 cm. The whole pipeline was also encased in a waterproof concrete jacket approximately 38 cm in cross-section (figure 30). It has been a source of interest and controversy for many years and even the origin

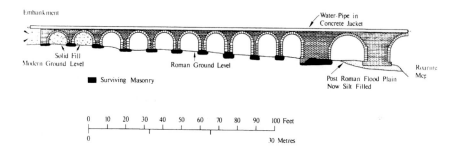

31. A drawing of the suggested bridge carrying the Lincoln aqueduct over the dip north of the city. (Drawing by John Wacher and Adam Sharpe)

32. A view of the aqueduct at Dorchester (Dorset), clearly illustrating how it followed the contours around the hills, from left to right in the photograph.

of the water supplying the aqueduct remains a source of debate. It was once considered that the water was drawn from the Roaring Meg spring just north of Lincoln but this is 20 metres lower than the site of the upper city of Lindum and a system to raise the water to feed into the aqueduct would also have been required. An alternative suggestion is that the water was tapped from springs on the higher ground further north, with the aqueduct crossing over the dip adjacent to the Roaring Meg spring by means of a bridge structure (figure 31). Hydrostatic pressure would have effectively driven the water across this bridge and up to the city (the 'inverted siphon' hypothesis) and the encased pipe would have had to withstand considerable internal pressures to allow this to happen.

However, although the Lincoln aqueduct is one of the most impressive and technologically sophisticated of the Roman civic water supply systems in Britain, doubts continue to be expressed about whether it actually worked, or even flowed in the right direction! If the source of the water was from the limestone ridge in the Lincolnshire Wolds it seems surprising that no limescale deposits have yet been found in any of the pipes excavated.

The *civitas* capitals at Leicester, Dorchester and Wroxeter were supplied by channel aqueducts rather than pipes. The Dorchester example followed the contours to the north-west of the town, running for over 15 km at a gentle gradient of 1 in 1750 (figures 32 and 33). There were probably

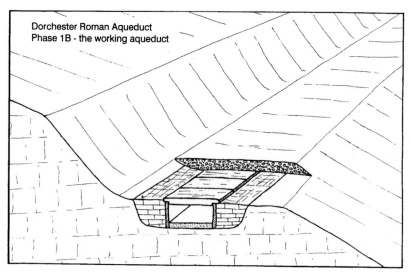

33. A cross-section of the Dorchester aqueduct, revealing the lined and covered water channel. (Drawing by Bill Putnam)

three channels and, although only one ever worked, it seems likely that the aqueduct could have supplied the requirements of the town. Unfortunately, channels are more liable to contamination throughout their course and, moreover, even though the favoured source of aqueduct water was from springs, the Dorchester aqueduct probably obtained most of its supply from a tributary of the river Frome at Frampton.

One of the most intriguing questions about aqueducts in the context of Roman Britain is why they were constructed anyway. There was certainly no shortage of water in Roman Britain, and in London, for example, the one hundred wells identified to date, in addition to the many natural springs, could easily have supplied all the city's drinking water requirements. Seventy-six wells have been identified at the extensively excavated site at Silchester and sixteen at Caerwent. Even at Lincoln a massive well sunk right through the limestone layers and into the lias clay at the site of the Roman forum would have served as a major source of water for the upper city. Perhaps the constantly running aqueducts found within Roman Britain were built more for supplying bath-houses and fountains or for flushing drains and latrines than for public water consumption.

By the imperial period aqueducts had also come to be regarded as one of the essential features of fully developed civilised urban life, and the existence of an aqueduct might say more about the aspirations of a provincial town to appear 'Roman' than any particular concern for

34. This modern fountain marks the end of the line of the Roman aqueduct in Dorchester.

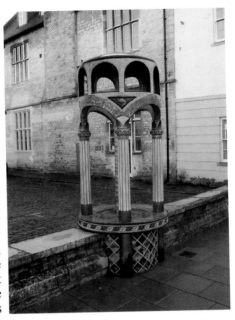

public health. Frontinus makes a revealing comment about the way Romans thought about aqueducts when he states: 'With these grand structures, so numerous and indispensable, carrying so many waters, who indeed would compare the idle Pyramids or the useless, although renowned, works of the Greeks?' The Lincoln and Dorchester examples would surely have been on the itinerary of any visiting imperial dignitary. Even today, the end of the route of the long-defunct Dorchester aqueduct is marked by an impressive reconstructed fountain that serves to remind us of the engineering prowess of our Roman forebears (figure 34).

Bath-houses are a ubiquitous feature of the Romanised world and, in Britain, are found in both towns and villas. As structures they can be viewed as another expression of Roman power and the adoption of Roman civilisation. However, although we might view the function of a bath-house as a cleansing establishment, the Romano-Briton may have used it for other purposes such as commerce, exercise, socialising, or medical

35. A view of the remains of the baths and exercise hall at Wroxeter (Shropshire). The entrance to the basilican exercise hall is still in place. (Photograph: © English Heritage)

treatment (figure 35). All four of the medical sects detailed in chapter 1 emphasised the key role of bathing in helping to restore health. However, treating patients in crowded bath-houses may also have contributed to the spread of infectious diseases, especially if the water was replaced infrequently.

Waste disposal

Visiting Chester a thousand years after the departure of the Romans, the monk Ranuph Higden wrote admiringly: 'There be ways under the ground vaulted marvellously with stonework, chambers having arched roofs overhead, huge stones engraved with the names of ancient men.' Even today, the sewage system in York can still be followed underground for 44 metres and there is evidence for side channels, manhole covers and sluices.

At Housesteads fort on Hadrian's Wall the Roman latrines can be clearly identified. The visible remains consist of a deep sewer flowing around a central platform and, as can be seen from the reconstruction, the sewer pit was spanned by a continuous row of lavatory seats (figures

36. The remains of the latrine at Housesteads on Hadrian's Wall, showing the deep sewer flowing around a central platform.

36 and 37). The small central water channel would have provided water for washing and it has been suggested that, in northern Britain, moss was used as a form of lavatory paper.

Effective waste disposal using sewers clearly depends on a plentiful supply of water and Frontinus emphasised the importance of aqueduct water in flushing the sewers of Rome. At Wroxeter there is evidence that the water from the open channel aqueduct was allowed to run off into the sewers. At Housesteads the location of the latrines at the lower south-east corner of the fort would have permitted surface water to be channelled in order to cleanse and wash the associated sewer.

Admittedly not all sewage systems were as impressive as those found at York, Lincoln or Chester. There are several examples of less dramatic affairs, such as the timber-lined drain running down the middle of the street in Cirencester, and these may have been more typical of many settlements in Roman Britain. However, latrines have been identified in small towns such as Malton (Yorkshire) as well as in the larger settlements at St Albans and Wroxeter.

Adopting a modern perspective, it is all too easy to be critical of the

37. A reconstructed view of the latrine at Housesteads illustrating the seating arrangements and the small central water channel for washing. (© English Heritage)

Roman waste-disposal arrangements. For example, there is evidence of cess-pits in close proximity to wells in York. At Caerleon the drain from the large latrine in a corner of the fortress was carried beside one of the barracks at only a shallow depth and, since the sides of the drain were very rough and the water supply came from a rainwater tank on the roof, there is little likelihood of faecal matter being properly carried away. Furthermore, although we understand the importance of good waste disposal in terms of removal and destruction of pathogenic microbes, the Romano-Britons may have been more concerned with removing foul smells. Often the drains extend only a short way out beyond the city walls and discharge into the town ditch or the nearest river.

However, a review of the bio-archaeological remains from the four *coloniae* at York, Chester, Gloucester and Colchester concluded that they must have been kept very clean. The state of the environment at York, for example, was in marked contrast to the situation in the later Viking or medieval city.

Houses and villas

Although we often associate the Romans with villas and towns, it is important to appreciate that in Roman Britain only about one per cent of the population lived in villas and 6.5 per cent in towns. Thus, for the majority of the residents of Roman Britain, life may have been very little different from that experienced by their forebears. In many cases the rural population initially continued to live in round houses along similar lines to their Iron Age ancestors. Such individuals would have continued to suffer from indoor pollution as a result of cohabitation with animals, cooking, and various cottage industries.

In the towns circumstances might might have been equally difficult for the poor, with their homes serving as both workshops and living quarters. In most towns it seems likely that only the rich could afford separate kitchens, piped water, private baths and private latrines. It is also probable that the congested layouts of the early towns of London and St Albans may have contributed to the devastating fires of AD 125 and 155. By analogy with the similar situation in seventeenth century London, it would not be unreasonable to suggest that the spread of disease could have also been a major problem. However, as Roman Britain developed, it seems likely that the urban housing stock also improved. Even in a small town such as Malton later house floors were either of beaten clay, *opus signinum* concrete or, occasionally, covered in mosaic. All of these surfaces would have been relatively easy to clean of refuse.

Burials

Romans generally disposed of their dead outside the city boundaries,

38. Two adjacent Roman barrows, or burial mounds, at Thornborough in Buckinghamshire. The larger is 4.9 metres high and 36 metres in diameter.

a practice that was also adopted in Roman Britain. Whatever the precise reasons behind this practice, it would undoubtedly have contributed to improving the public health by reducing the risk of disease transmission. In Lincoln, for example, where it has been estimated that there would have been 350 burials per year, the main cemeteries lay along the approach roads to the city. As is also the case from other sites in Roman Britain, the general impression is that the location and practice of burial was orderly and well organised.

Some individuals were interred in more substantial structures and roadside barrows are more common in Roman Britain than the stone tombs found elsewhere in the empire (figure 38).

7
Conclusion

On the southern side of the Lleyn peninsula is the village of Llangian. In the ancient churchyard, nestling among the monuments of the more recently departed, lies the tombstone of a doctor. The monolithic pillar can be seen near the church wall and the clearly legible inscription (figure 39) reads: 'MELI MEDICI FILI MARTINI ICIT' ('the stone of Melus, the doctor, son of Martinus'). The stone has been dated to the late fifth century and perhaps represents the last remnant of medical care in Roman Britain.

In looking back at medicine and health care within Roman Britain it seems likely that many of the treatments used were probably ineffective and some even dangerous. Clearly there would also have been marked inequalities in health and in access to medical care in Roman Britain. It is also impossible to ascertain whether the constructions we consider nowadays as essential to maintaining the public health were built by the Romano-Britons with health as the primary objective. It has even been suggested that the Car Dyke might have reduced the incidence of malaria in Roman Britain but, even if true, this was surely not the main reason for draining the marshes around the Wash.

However, it would be wrong for us to dismiss the Roman approach

39. The tombstone of Melus, dating from the late fifth century, in the churchyard at Llangian on the Lleyn peninsula in Gwynedd.

to health care and to assume that we have got it entirely right today. Nowadays, many patients who consult their general practitioner are suffering from symptoms that are often due to the stresses and strains of modern life. Over-investigation of such somatic symptoms as fatigue, dizziness or headaches can cause considerable harm. Suggesting that such patients spend a quiet week resting, bathing and taking occasional brisk walks with the dogs in a place such as Lydney would perhaps be of greater benefit!

In conclusion it seems likely that Britain was a healthier place under Roman rule than had it been previously or would be again for several hundred years after the death of Melus.

Further reading

Alcock, J. P. *Food in Roman Britain*. Tempus, 2001.

Baker, P. A. *Medical Care for the Roman Army on the Rhine, Danube and British Frontiers in the First, Second and Early Third Centuries AD*. British Archaeological Reports, 2004.

Boon, G. C. *Roman Silchester*. Parrish, 1957.

Bowman, A. K. *Life and Letters on the Roman Frontier*. British Museum Publications, 1994.

Cunliffe, B. *Roman Bath Discovered*. Tempus, 2000.

Cruse, A. *Roman Medicine*. Tempus, 2004.

De la Bédoyère, G. *The Buildings of Roman Britain*. Tempus, 2001.

Eisinger, J. 'Lead and wine. Eberhard Gockel and the *colica Pictonum*', *Medical History* 26 (1982), 279–302.

Hart, G. D. *Asclepius: the God of Medicine*. Royal Society of Medicine Press, 2001.

Jackson, R. *Doctors and Diseases in the Roman Empire*. British Museum Publications, 1988.

Jackson, R. 'A new collyrium stamp from Cambridge and a correct reading of the stamp from Caistor-by-Norwich', *Britannia* 21 (1990), 275–283.

Jones, M. J. *Roman Lincoln*. Tempus, 2002.

King, H. *Greek and Roman Medicine*. Duckworth, 2003.

Nutton, V. *Ancient Medicine*. Routledge, 2004.

Penn, R. G. *Medicine on Ancient Greek and Roman Coins*. Seaby, 1994.

Putnam, B. *The Romans (Discover Dorset)*. Dovecote, 2000.

Roberts, C., and Cox, M. *Health and Disease in Britain*. Sutton, 2003.

Scarborough, J. *Roman Medicine*. Thames & Hudson, 1969.

Toynbee, J. M. C. *Death and Burial in the Roman World*. Thames & Hudson, 1971.

Voinot, J. *Les Cachets à collyres dans le monde romain* (Monographies Instrumentum 7). Montagnac, 1999.

Wacher, J. *The Towns of Roman Britain*. Routledge, 1995.

White, R., and Barker, P. *Wroxeter: Life and Death of a Roman City*. Tempus, 1999.

Wright, T. *Uriconium: An Account of the Ancient Roman City of Wroxeter*. London, 1872.

Museums and sites

Ashmolean Museum, Beaumont Street, Oxford OX1 2PH. Telephone: 01865 278000. Website: www.ashmolean.org (Roman medical instruments, collyrium stamp.)

Brading Roman Villa, Morton Old Road, Brading, Isle of Wight PO36 0EN. Telephone: 01983 406223. Website: www.bradingromanvilla.org.uk (Villa, museum, eye needle.)

The British Museum, Great Russell Street, London WC1B 3DG. Telephone: 020 7323 8000. Website: www.thebritishmuseum.ac.uk (Roman medical instruments, collyrium stamps, Wroxeter golden eyes.)

Chesters Fort, Chollerford, Northumberland NE46 4EE. Telephone: 01434 681379. Website: www.english-heritage.org.uk (Bath-house, museum.)

Colchester Castle Museum, Castle Park, Colchester, Essex CO1 1TJ. Telephone: 01206 282939. Website: www.colchestermuseums.org.uk (Medical instruments from Stanway, collyrium stamps.)

Corinium Museum, Park Street, Cirencester, Gloucestershire GL7 2BX. Telephone: 01285 655611. Website: www.cotswold.gov.uk (Collyrium stamp.)

Dorchester, Dorset. (Aqueduct. Not much of the route is accessible but a view of it can be had where the railway enters a cutting at Poundbury, NGR SY 683912.)

Grosvenor Museum, Grosvenor Street, Chester CH1 2DD. Telephone: 01244 402008. Website: www.grosvenormuseum.ac.uk (Altars, collyrium stamp.)

Housesteads Fort, Bardon Mill, Northumberland NE47 6NN. Telephone: 01434 344363. Website: www.nationaltrust.org.uk (Hospital, latrines, museum.)

Lincoln Museum, Danes Terrace, Lincoln LN2 1LP. Telephone: 01522 550990. Website: www.thecollection.lincoln.museum (Aqueduct pipe.)

Lydney. Private site but enquiries can be made via the Estate Office, Park Farmhouse, Old Park, Lydney, Gloucestershire GL15 6BU. Telephone: 01594 845497. Website: www.gloucestershire.gov.uk (Temple complex, bath-house, museum, collyrium stamp.)

Museum of Antiquities, The University, Newcastle upon Tyne NE1 7RU. Telephone: 0191 222 7846. Website: http://museums.ncl.ac.uk (Tombstone from Housesteads.)

Museum of London, 150 London Wall, London EC2Y 5HN. Telephone: 0870 444 3857. Website: www.museumoflondon.org.uk (Roman medical instruments, collyrium stamp.)

Newport Museum, John Frost Square, Newport, South Wales NP20 1PA. Telephone: 01633 656656. Website: www.newport.gov.uk (Uvula forceps.)

Norwich Castle Museum, The Castle, Norwich, Norfolk NR1 3JU. Telephone: 01603 493625. Website: www.museums.norfolk.gov.uk (Uterine sound.)

The Old Fulling Mill Museum of Archaeology, Old Fulling Mill, The Banks, Durham DH1 3EB. Telephone: 0191 334 1823. Website: www.dur.ac.uk/fulling.mill (Altar from Binchester.)

Roman Baths and Museum, Pump Room, Stall Street, Bath, Somerset BA1 1LZ. Telephone: 01225 477785. Website: www.romanbaths.co.uk (Bathing complex, hot spring, temple precinct, altars.)

Vindolanda Fort Museum, Bardon Mill, Hexham, Northumberland NE47 7JN. Telephone: 01434 344277. Website: www.vindolanda.com (Writing tablets, eye patch.)

Wroxeter Roman City, Shrewsbury, Shropshire SY5 6PH. Telephone: 01743 761330. Website: www.english-heritage.org.uk (Museum, baths and exercise hall.)

Yorkshire Museum, Museum Gardens, York YO1 7FR. Telephone: 01904 687687. Website: www.yorkshiremuseum.org.uk (Collyrium stamp.)

56

Index

Page numbers in italic refer to illustrations